THE SECRETS TO KNOW BEFORE INVESTING

MASTER KEY TO GENERATIONAL WEALTH

BY

DONALD BUFFET

THE CONCEPT INVESTMENT

Investing entails allocating money, resources, or capital to acquire assets, ventures, or financial instruments with the anticipation of generating income, appreciation, or returns over time, aligning with specific financial objectives. It is a widely adopted means to amass wealth and achieve financial goals, contingent upon factors like financial position, risk tolerance, investment objectives, and time horizon.

Diverse forms of investment include financial instruments like stocks, bonds, mutual funds, and real estate, as well as business investments, commodities, and alternative assets such as private equity, venture capital, and cryptocurrencies. The central aim is to secure a return on invested capital, encompassing capital appreciation, income (like dividends or rental payments), or a blend of both. Investors evaluate elements such as risk tolerance, expected returns, liquidity, and investment horizon when selecting options.

While investments offer opportunities, they inherently carry risks with no guaranteed returns. Fluctuations occur based on market conditions, economic factors, and individual performance. Investors are advised to conduct thorough research, diversify portfolios, and seek professional advice to manage risks effectively. Here are some general investment options and strategies:

Stock Market: Investing in individual stocks or ETFs for potential capital appreciation. Diversify to mitigate risk.

Bonds: Less risky than stocks, bonds provide fixed interest payments over a specified period, offering stability and income.

Mutual Funds: Pooled funds managed by professionals, suitable for those preferring a hands-off approach.

Real Estate: Offers income and appreciation; consider properties for rental income or Real Estate Investment Trusts (REITs).

Index Funds: Mirror-specific market indices, providing broad market exposure with low fees and passive management.

Diversification: Spread investments across various asset classes and sectors to reduce risk.

Dollar-Cost Averaging: Consistently invest fixed amounts at regular intervals, potentially mitigating market timing impact.

Retirement Accounts: Contribute to tax-advantaged accounts like 401(k)s or IRAs for long-term wealth building.

Education Savings Accounts: Invest in accounts like 529 plans with tax advantages for children's education expenses.

Consult a Financial Advisor: Seek personalized advice to assess your situation and recommend suitable strategies.

Investing demands diligent research, goal understanding, and risk evaluation before making decisions.

NUMEROUS MEANING OF INVESTMENT TO KNOW

Investing entails allocating money, resources, or capital to a project, business, or financial instrument with the expectation of generating income or profit over time.

It is the strategic process of purchasing assets such as stocks, bonds, real estate, or commodities to realize a return on the invested capital.

Investment involves a deliberate decision to save and allocate funds for achieving long-term financial goals and enhancing wealth.

It's the committed act of putting money or resources into a venture or opportunity to reap potential financial returns or benefits.

Investing denotes the acquisition of assets or securities to generate income through dividends, interest, rent, or capital appreciation.

It encompasses setting aside funds or resources for engaging in productive or income-generating activities and anticipating future financial rewards.

Investment signifies the intentional deployment of funds into diverse financial instruments or assets to foster financial growth or preserve wealth.

It's the act of placing money into a specific project, business, or financial vehicle with the expectation of earning a positive return on the initial capital.

Investment involves a strategic decision to allocate financial resources to participate in economic activities that have the potential to generate profits or increase value.

It's the process of exchanging money or assets for securities, properties, or other financial instruments to generate income or appreciation.

Investing signifies the act of buying, holding, or trading financial instruments or assets to generate wealth, build assets, or secure future financial stability.

It requires the commitment of financial resources or capital with the expectation of achieving capital gains, income, or other financial benefits over a specified period.

Investing is the act of placing money, time, or effort into an enterprise, venture, or asset class to gain a return or profit.

It involves making informed decisions to allocate funds or resources to different investment options or opportunities, aiming to maximize returns while managing risks.

Investing is the act of converting savings or surplus funds into assets, properties, or financial instruments to generate income or appreciation over time.

The practice of purchasing financial securities, shares, or assets to capitalize on market opportunities and earn a positive return on investment.

Investing necessitates the commitment of resources to various financial instruments or projects, based on careful analysis and evaluation of potential risks and rewards.

It is the act of entrusting capital or funds into different avenues or assets with the expectation of obtaining financial gains or benefits in the future.

Investing is the deliberate act of placing money or assets into ventures, businesses, or financial products to achieve long-term financial goals or objectives.

The process of allocating financial resources to acquire assets or securities to preserve or increase the value of the invested capital.

WHAT IS SHORT-TERM INVESTMENTS?

Short-time investments are financial assets held for a relatively short duration, typically spanning from a few days to a few years. Unlike long-term investments, focused on extended holdings, short-term investments prioritize generating returns over a concise timeframe. The concept of short-term investment varies but generally involves strategies emphasizing liquidity, swift returns, and lower risk than long-term options. This section will delve into the meaning of short-term investments, examining their key traits and benefits.

Key Characteristics of Short-Term Investments
1. Liquidity:

Advantage: Short-term investments boast high liquidity, easily converted into cash without significant loss.
Examples: Money market accounts, Treasury bills, and certificates of deposit.
2. Low Risk:

Advantage: Generally involves lower risk compared to long-term investments, less exposed to market volatility.
Examples: High-quality corporate bonds, and short-term government securities.
3. Quick Returns:

Advantage: Geared towards providing fast returns, aiming for income or capital gains within a shorter period.
Comparison: Contrasts with long-term investments, where returns may take years to materialize.
4. Diversification:

Strategy: Integral for well-diversified portfolios, balancing risk and return.

Mix: Short-term investments for stability and liquidity, long-term for potentially higher returns.

Examples of Short-Term Investments

Money Market Funds

Short-Term Bonds

Treasury Bills

Commercial Paper

Bank Savings Accounts

Considerations and Risks

1. Lower Potential Returns:

Consideration: Short-term investments tend to yield lower returns compared to long-term counterparts.

Trade-off: Emphasis on stability and liquidity may sacrifice the potential for higher growth.

2. Interest Rate Risk:

Concern: Susceptibility to interest rate fluctuations, impacting the value of fixed-income securities.

Mitigation: Monitoring interest rate trends is crucial for adjusting strategies.

3. Inflation Risk:

Challenge: Low returns on short-term investments may not keep pace with inflation.

Evaluation: Investors must assess whether returns will be sufficient considering the potential inflation impact.

While short-term investments offer advantages, awareness of associated considerations and risks is crucial for informed decision-making and effective expectation management.

WHAT IS LONG-TERM INVESTMENT?

Long-term investments play a pivotal role in the realm of financial planning for individuals, businesses, and institutions, aiming to fulfill financial objectives over an extended period. Unlike their short-term counterparts, which prioritize immediate gains, long-term investments are strategically crafted to offer sustained financial security and growth, often spanning several years or even decades. This approach centers on allocating funds to assets poised for significant appreciation, thus yielding substantial returns. This article delves into the essential characteristics, advantages, and considerations associated with long-term investments.

Characteristics of Long-Term Investments
1. Time Horizon:

Definition: Characterized by an extended time horizon, long-term investments involve committing capital to assets like stocks, bonds, real estate, or mutual funds.
Benefits: The prolonged time frame allows for weathering short-term fluctuations and harnessing the power of compounding returns.
2. Potential for Higher Returns:

Advantage: Long-term investments offer the potential for superior returns compared to short-term counterparts.
Mechanism: Investing in historically growth-oriented assets allows for compounding returns, creating a snowball effect and enhancing overall return on investment.
3. Diversification:

Strategy: Emphasis on diversification helps mitigate risk by spreading investments across various asset classes, industries, or regions.
Rationale: This strategy safeguards portfolios, ensuring that gains from some investments can offset losses in others.
Benefits of Long-Term Investments
1. Wealth Accumulation:

Opportunity: Long-term investments enable gradual wealth accumulation by consistently investing in a diversified portfolio.
Impact: The compounding effect contributes to substantial wealth, facilitating the achievement of financial goals like retirement planning or education funding.
2. Capital Appreciation:

Potential: Assets such as stocks and real estate in long-term investments have significant potential for appreciation.
Strategy: Investing in growth-oriented sectors or emerging markets enhances the prospect of substantial returns upon eventual liquidation.
3. Income Generation:

Source: Long-term investments can provide a consistent income stream through dividends, bonds, rental properties, or interest-bearing accounts.
Utility: Passive income can be reinvested to expedite wealth accumulation or utilized to cover expenses, improving overall financial stability.
Considerations for Long-Term Investments
1. Risk Tolerance:

Reality: Long-term investments are not immune to risk, including market volatility and economic downturns.
Guideline: Investors must assess their risk tolerance, aligning investment choices with their comfort level.
2. Research and Due Diligence:

Imperative: Thorough research, historical performance evaluation, and market trend analysis are crucial before committing to long-term investments.
Enhancement: Seeking professional advice empowers investors to make informed decisions based on comprehensive information.
In essence, long-term investments serve as a cornerstone in building financial prosperity, necessitating strategic planning, diversification, and a comprehensive understanding of associated risks and rewards.

USEFULNESS OF INVESTMENT

Investing presents a range of advantages for individuals aiming to expand their wealth, attain financial objectives, and fortify their future. Here are the key benefits associated with investment:

1. Wealth Accumulation:
Investing enables potential wealth growth over time. Allocating funds to diverse vehicles like stocks, bonds, real estate, or mutual funds provides the opportunity to outpace inflation, thereby increasing overall net worth.

2. Income Generation:
Many investments yield regular income through dividends, interest, or rental payments. Assets like dividend-paying stocks, bonds, or real estate can supply a consistent income stream, complementing salary or other revenue sources.

3. Capital Appreciation:
Investments in assets like stocks or real estate hold the potential for capital appreciation. As these assets increase in value over time, investors can capitalize on the appreciation by selling for a profit if desired.

4. Diversification:
Investing allows for portfolio diversification across different asset classes, sectors, or regions. This risk mitigation strategy enhances overall risk-adjusted returns by reducing dependence on a single investment.

5. Inflation Protection:
Investing acts as a hedge against inflation, preserving and increasing the real value of wealth. Assets that outpace inflation contribute to maintaining purchasing power over time.

6. Retirement Planning:
Crucial for retirement planning, investing in accounts like 401(k)s or IRAs enables individuals to accumulate funds gradually, ensuring financial security during non-working years.

7. Tax Advantages:
Certain investments offer tax advantages. Retirement accounts, such as IRAs and 401(k)s, provide tax deductions or tax-free growth, aiding investors in minimizing their tax liability and optimizing their financial situation.

8. Portfolio Customization:
Investing empowers individuals to tailor portfolios to specific goals, risk tolerance, and preferences. A diverse array of investment options

and strategies allows for the creation of a portfolio aligned with financial objectives.

9. Financial Independence:
Successful investing can lead to financial independence, where accumulated wealth sustains the desired lifestyle without sole reliance on employment income. This freedom offers increased flexibility and peace of mind.

10. Legacy Planning:
Investments can form part of an estate plan, allowing individuals to pass on financial legacies to future generations or charitable causes.

It's crucial to acknowledge that investing involves risks, and returns are not guaranteed. Before making investment decisions, individuals should thoroughly assess their financial situation, goals, and risk tolerance. Seeking guidance from a financial advisor provides personalized insights based on individual circumstances.

APPROPRIATE TIME TO INVEST

Determining the optimal time for investment poses a challenge, given the multifaceted influences and inherent unpredictability of financial markets. Nonetheless, several guiding principles can aid in decision-making:

Embrace the Long Term: Opting for a long-term investment perspective helps cushion the impact of short-term market fluctuations. The duration of your investment often surpasses the significance of precisely timing market entry or exit. Staying committed over an extended period allows for potential benefits from the compounding growth of your investments.

Commence Early: Initiating investments sooner translates to more time for your investments to mature. Time plays a pivotal role in wealth accumulation, leveraging the compounding effect where returns generate additional returns over an extended period.

Craft a Financial Plan: Establish a comprehensive financial plan before delving into investments. Clearly outline your financial objectives, whether they involve retirement savings, home acquisition, or funding education. Identify your risk tolerance, time horizon, and comfortable investment amount, aligning your investments with specific goals.

Avoid Market Timing: Shunning attempts to predict short-term market shifts and eschewing market-timing strategies proves prudent. Consistently identifying market lows and highs is challenging. Instead, concentrate on long-term trends and the fundamentals of your prospective investments.

Dollar-Cost Averaging: Employ the strategy of dollar-cost averaging by consistently investing a fixed amount irrespective of market conditions. This approach mitigates the impact of short-term market volatility, allowing for the purchase of more shares during price lows and fewer shares during peaks.

Stay Informed: Stay abreast of financial news, market trends, and economic indicators. While refraining from impulsive decisions based on short-term market movements, a general understanding of the investment landscape aids informed decision-making.

Acknowledge Risks: Recognize that investing inherently entails risks, and perfect timing is elusive. Prioritize evaluating your circumstances, goals, and risk tolerance before making investment decisions. Seeking guidance from a financial advisor tailored to your specific situation can be invaluable.

CAN EVERYONE INVEST?

Investing is generally open to anyone with financial means, though specific requirements may exist for certain options. Key groups of investors include:

1. Individuals: Most adults can invest in diverse options like stocks, bonds, real estate, and more.

2. Minors: Minors can invest with custodians or guardians managing their investments until they reach adulthood.

3. Retirement Savers: Those planning for retirement can utilize accounts like 401(k)s and IRAs, offering tax advantages for long-term savings.

4. Business Owners: Business owners can invest in their ventures, and other businesses, or diversify outside their enterprises.

5. Institutional Investors: Entities like pension funds and hedge funds pool large capital amounts for diversified asset investments.

6. Non-profit Organizations: Nonprofits may invest for income or endowment growth, aligning with their mission.

7. Government Entities: Governments invest funds for purposes like infrastructure development or pension funds.

While accessible to all, specific investment options vary based on factors like residency, regulations, and financial circumstances. Thorough research and professional advice are recommended before committing funds.

RIGHT PLACE TO INVEST

Choosing where to invest depends on factors like goals, risk tolerance, and knowledge. Consider these avenues:

1. Stock Market: Invest in individual stocks or ETFs to own shares of publicly traded companies.

2. Bonds: Explore government, corporate, or municipal bonds offering fixed interest payments.

3. Mutual Funds and Index Funds: Pool money with others for diversified portfolios managed by professionals.

4. Real Estate: Invest in properties, REITs, or real estate crowdfunding for rental income and appreciation.

5. ETFs: Tradeable funds providing exposure to various assets for diversification and flexibility.

6. Retirement Accounts: Utilize 401(k)s or IRAs for tax advantages and long-term wealth building.

7. Commodities: Consider gold, silver, or other commodities for diversification and inflation hedging.

8. Peer-to-peer Lending: Lend money through platforms for potentially higher returns, albeit with higher risks.

9. Startup Investments: Venture into early-stage startups for high-risk, high-reward opportunities.

10. Education and Self-Development: Invest in education and skills for long-term career and income benefits.

Diversify across asset classes, aligning investments with goals and seeking professional advice.

PLACES NOT TO INVEST
Despite diverse opportunities, caution is essential in certain areas:

1. High-risk Speculative Investments: Beware of high-return promises with minimal risk, such as certain cryptocurrencies or penny stocks.

2. Pyramid and Ponzi Schemes: Steer clear of fraudulent schemes relying on new investors to pay existing ones.

3. Unregulated or Illegal Investments: Avoid investments outside regulatory oversight or involving illegal activities.

4. Get-rich-quick Schemes: Be skeptical of investments promising quick, substantial returns with minimal effort.

5. High-cost and Complex Products: Watch out for products with high fees or complexity that can impact returns.

6. Unfamiliar or Speculative Markets: Exercise caution in unfamiliar or speculative markets, like cryptocurrency or specialized industries.

7. Debt-driven Investments: Be wary of excessive borrowing or margin trading, as high debt levels amplify risks.

8. Individual Stocks Without Research: Investigate before investing in individual stocks to understand specific company risks.

9. Emotional or Impulsive Investments: Avoid decisions driven by emotions, market hype, or short-term trends.

10. Investments Without Due Diligence: Conduct thorough due diligence to avoid opaque or questionable investments.

Investing carries risks, requiring careful assessment and, if needed, guidance from financial professionals.

WHO TO MANAGE YOUR INVESTMENT

There are diverse options for handling investments, contingent on your preferences, knowledge, and the intricacy of your investment strategy. Explore these common approaches:

Self-Management: If you possess the knowledge and confidence, managing your investments independently can be cost-effective. This involves thorough research, staying abreast of market trends, and actively monitoring and rebalancing your portfolio.

Financial Advisors: Collaborating with a professional financial advisor provides expertise in managing investments. They assist in crafting a tailored investment plan aligned with your goals, offer ongoing portfolio management, and guide asset allocation, investment selection, and risk management.

Robo-Advisors: These digital platforms utilize algorithms to automate investment management. By assessing your risk profile and goals, robo-advisors create and manage a diversified portfolio of ETFs, offering a cost-effective solution for automated portfolio management.

Mutual Fund Managers: Investing in mutual funds grants access to professional fund managers who make investment decisions on behalf of investors. Fund managers conduct research, select securities, and manage holdings in line with the fund's objectives.

Institutional Investment Managers: Institutional investors, like pension funds or insurance companies, either maintain in-house investment teams or outsource management to professional asset firms. These managers handle large fund pools, employing tailored strategies to meet specific goals.

Family Office: High-net-worth individuals or families may establish a family office—a dedicated team managing investments, financial affairs, and wealth planning. Family offices offer comprehensive, customized investment management services.

Consider your investment knowledge, complexity of needs, and time availability when deciding who will manage your investments. Evaluate the qualifications, track record, and fees associated with any professional you consider.

Regardless of your chosen approach, staying informed, regularly reviewing investments, and reassessing financial goals and risk tolerance are crucial for successful investment management.

THE RIGHT PARTNERS IN INVESTMENT

When exploring partnership opportunities in the realm of investment, numerous entities or professionals are available for potential collaboration. The decision hinges on your specific investment needs, goals, and desired level of involvement. Here are some potential partners to contemplate:

Financial Advisors: Collaborating with a financial advisor offers personalized guidance and expertise in crafting an investment strategy aligned with your goals and risk tolerance. They provide recommendations, monitor investments, and offer ongoing advice for informed decision-making.

Investment Managers: Investment management firms or professionals specialize in overseeing investment portfolios for individuals or institutions. They possess expertise in various asset classes and manage day-to-day investment activities to align with your objectives.

Real Estate Agents or Brokers: For those interested in real estate investment, partnering with a knowledgeable agent or broker provides access to potential properties, market insights, and negotiation assistance. They facilitate property discovery and guide through real estate transactions.

Venture Capitalists or Angel Investors: Considering investments in startups or early-stage companies? Partnering with venture capitalists or angel investors grants access to opportunities, industry expertise, and networks. They often invest in promising startups and provide mentorship to entrepreneurs.

Private Equity Firms: Private equity firms invest in privately held companies and can collaborate to pool capital for large-scale projects. They offer expertise in business management, growth strategies, and access to industry contacts.

Peer Networks or Investment Groups: Joining investment clubs, online communities, or networking groups allows collaboration with like-minded individuals. These networks foster knowledge sharing, idea generation, and potential co-investment opportunities.

Financial Institutions: Reputable banks, brokerage firms, or investment platforms may provide investment services. Partnering with them gives access to a variety of investment options, research, and tools.

Legal and Tax Professionals: Consulting legal and tax professionals is crucial for compliance, understanding the legal framework, and optimizing tax strategy. They guide in structuring investments, tax planning, and addressing legal considerations.

Business Partners or Co-Investors: Forming partnerships or co-investing with individuals who share similar goals allows pooling resources, expertise sharing, and risk mitigation, especially for larger-scale investments or projects.

When seeking an investment partner, assess qualifications, track record, reputation, and alignment with your objectives. Evaluate partnership terms, including roles, responsibilities, and any associated fees or profit-sharing arrangements. It's important to note that partnering does not guarantee success, and thorough due diligence, research, and informed decision-making based on financial circumstances are essential.

RISKS OF INVESTMENT

Investing entails various risks that demand investor awareness for informed decision-making. Key risks associated with investments include:

Market Risk: The potential loss of investment value due to general market fluctuations influenced by economic conditions, geopolitical events, interest rates, and investor sentiment.

Volatility Risk: The likelihood of significant price fluctuations, especially in high-volatility investments like stocks or certain cryptocurrencies, leading to substantial gains or losses.

Credit Risk: The risk of a borrower defaulting on debt obligations, applicable when investing in bonds or providing loans, potentially resulting in non-payment or delayed payments.

Inflation Risk: The risk that rising inflation erodes the purchasing power of investments over time, especially if returns don't outpace inflation.

Liquidity Risk: The challenge of buying or selling certain investments quickly without significant costs or delays, often associated with illiquid assets like real estate or specific private equity holdings.

Concentration Risk: The impact of having a substantial portion of the portfolio concentrated in a single asset, sector, or geographic region, which can disproportionately affect overall performance.

Political and Regulatory Risk: Uncertainties introduced by political and regulatory changes that can impact specific industries or investments.

Currency Risk: Fluctuations in exchange rates affect the value of foreign assets when converting them back to the home currency.

Interest Rate Risk: Changes in interest rates impact the value of fixed-income investments, such as bonds, with prices falling as rates rise and vice versa.

Operational and Counterparty Risk: Potential losses due to operational failures or disruptions within financial institutions, and the risk that a counterparty fails to fulfill its transactional obligations.

It's crucial to recognize that different investments carry varying levels of risk. Higher-risk investments offer the potential for greater returns but come with increased volatility and potential losses. Before investing, assess your risk tolerance, objectives, and specific risks associated with the investment. Diversification, thorough research, and staying informed help mitigate risks. Consulting a financial advisor provides personalized guidance aligned with your circumstances.

PROTECTING YOUR INVESTMENT

Securing your investments is crucial for preserving your capital and managing risks effectively. Here are essential steps to safeguard your investments:

Diversify Your Portfolio: Spread investments across different asset classes, industries, and regions to minimize the impact of market fluctuations on your overall portfolio.

Set Clear Goals and Risk Tolerance: Define your investment goals and assess your risk tolerance to align your decisions with a well-defined plan.

Thorough Research: Before investing, conduct comprehensive research on historical performance, market trends, financial health, and associated risks.

Stay Informed: Keep abreast of market news, economic trends, and relevant developments that may influence your investments.

Regularly Review and Rebalance: Periodically review and rebalance your portfolio to maintain alignment with your goals and risk tolerance.

Avoid Emotional Decision-Making: Steer clear of impulsive actions driven by market fluctuations; adhere to a long-term investment strategy.

Understand Fees and Costs: Be aware of associated fees, opting for lower-cost alternatives when suitable to maximize returns.

Monitor Performance and Statements: Regularly review investment performance and statements, addressing any discrepancies promptly.

Consider Professional Advice: Seek guidance from a qualified financial advisor if you're uncertain or lack expertise in managing investments.

Guard Against Fraud: Exercise caution against investment scams, protecting your information and investing only with reputable institutions.

Remember, successful investing involves assessing and managing risks while staying informed about market dynamics.

LAWS OF INVESTMENT

While there's no definitive list of investment laws, these principles guide successful investors:

Diversification: Spread risk across asset classes, industries, and regions.
Long-Term Focus: Benefit from compounding growth and ride out short-term fluctuations.
Risk and Return: Higher returns come with higher risk.
Thorough Research: Investigate assets before investing.
Clear Strategy: Develop an investment plan aligned with goals and risk tolerance.
Avoid Complexity: Steer clear of speculative investments without proper understanding.
Emotional Control: Avoid impulsive decisions based on short-term market movements.

Fundamentals First: Focus on earnings, cash flow, and valuation.
Avoid Overtrading: Regularly review but avoid excessive changes based on market noise.
Fee Awareness: Consider fees' impact on returns; opt for low-cost options.
How to Plan Investment
Effective investment planning involves these key steps:

Set Financial Goals: Clearly define short and long-term financial objectives.
Assess Risk Tolerance: Evaluate comfort with investment ups and downs.
Define Time Horizon: Align investments with goal timelines.
Determine Capital: Assess funds available after accounting for expenses.
Educate Yourself: Understand investment options, risks, and potential returns.
Asset Allocation: Distribute capital among different asset classes.
Select Investments: Research and choose specific investments within each class.
Monitor and Review: Regularly assess performance and market trends.
Discipline Over Emotion: Stick to the plan; avoid emotional decisions.
Professional Advice: Consult a financial advisor if needed.
Investment planning is dynamic; regularly revisit and adjust based on changing circumstances.

SOURCES OF CAPITAL FOR INVESTMENT

Personal Savings: Accumulate funds by saving a portion of your income.
Investment Income: Reinvest earnings from existing investments.
Budgeting: Optimize spending to free up funds for investment.
Selling Assets: Sell unused or appreciated assets for capital.
Loans: Consider personal loans or home equity options cautiously.
Crowdfunding: Explore online platforms for capital from a large number of individuals.
Family and Friends: Approach close contacts for investment or loans with clear terms.
Angel Investors: Seek funding for business ideas from investors or venture capitalists.
Government Programs: Investigate grants or programs supporting specific investments.
Retirement Funds: Explore options within regulations, considering tax implications.
Evaluate costs, risks, and terms before deciding, ensuring alignment with your investment goals. Consult a financial advisor for personalized guidance based on your circumstances.

SECTORS TO INVEST

Here is a compilation of sectors worth considering for investment:

Technology and Software

Healthcare and Pharmaceuticals

Financial Services and Banking

Renewable Energy

E-commerce and Online Retail

Telecommunications

Artificial Intelligence and Machine Learning

Electric Vehicles and Clean
Transportation

Consumer Goods and Retail

Biotechnology

Real Estate and Property Development

Cybersecurity

Aerospace and Defense

Robotics and Automation

Sustainable Agriculture

Entertainment and Media

Education Technology

Water and Environmental Services

Infrastructure and Construction

Gaming and Esports

Internet of Things (IoT)

Renewable Fuels

Logistics and Supply Chain

Clean Energy Technology

Fintech (Financial Technology)

HealthTech

Smart Cities

Insurance

Travel and Tourism

Nanotechnology

Keep in mind that this list is not exhaustive, and the performance of each sector can vary. Thorough research, assessment of market conditions, and consideration of your investment objectives and risk tolerance are crucial when making investment decisions. Consulting with a financial advisor can offer personalized advice based on your specific circumstances and goals.

www.ingramcontent.com/pod-product-compliance
Lightning Source LLC
Chambersburg PA
CBHW080947260726
48661CB00010B/4140